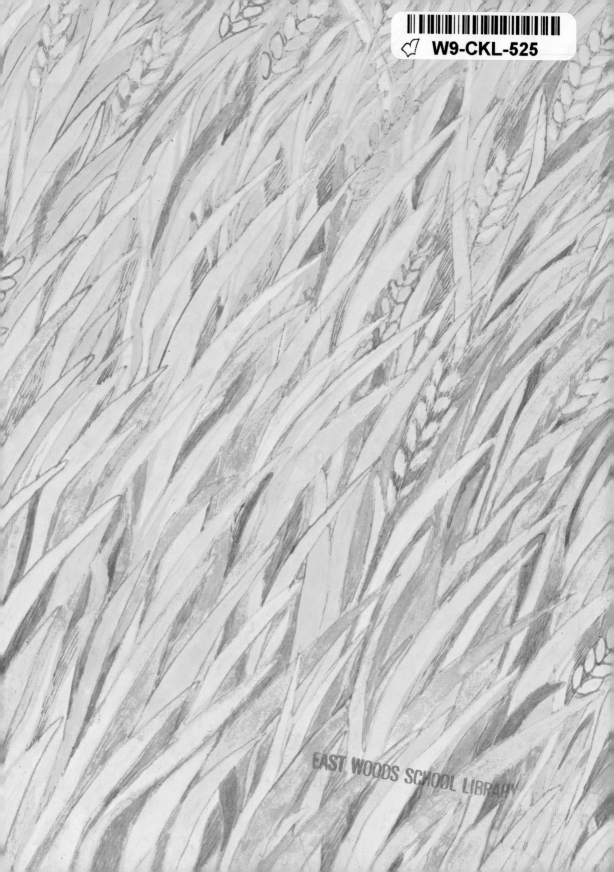

A HAMSTER'S JOURNEY

A HAMSTER'S JOURNEY

by
Luis Murschetz

Translation by Harry Allard

Prentice-Hall, Inc. / Englewood Cliffs / New Jersey

Printed in the United States of America   •J

Prentice-Hall International, Inc., London
Prentice-Hall of Australia, Pty. Ltd., North Sydney
Prentice-Hall of Canada, Ltd., Toronto
Prentice-Hall of India Private Ltd., New Delhi
Prentice-Hall of Japan, Inc., Tokyo

10   9   8   7   6   5   4   3   2   1

Library of Congress Cataloging in Publication Data

Murschetz, Luis.
  A hamster's journey.

    Translation of Der Hamster Radel.
    SUMMARY: The pet hamsters in a small
town take to the road on wheels to escape captivity.
    [1.   Hamsters—Fiction]   I.   Title.
PZ7.M9672Ham3   [E]   76-9788
ISBN 0-13-372383-6

For Annette

Wheeler the Hamster lived in a drugstore window. He ran in his little wheel all day long, not even stopping for lunch. Passersby who watched him run would remember their aches and pains and step inside the store to buy cough medicine or vitamins or a hot-water bottle.

"Run, run, run!" the fat druggist barked whenever Wheeler would stop to catch his breath. "Come on, run for your supper, Wheeler!" the druggist shouted and threw Wheeler a few kernels of grain that smelled like cough medicine and tasted like milk of magnesia—phewy! Wheeler was so lonely and so unhappy. "Was it his fate," he asked himself, "to keep running, running, running for the rest of his life?"

But then one day something awful happened. The ladder gave way under the fat druggist as he was piling some pills on the top shelf. He crashed through the drugstore window, and Wheeler the Hamster flew out in his little wheel.

Scared half to death, Wheeler began to run, his little wheel rolling down the street faster and faster. The grownups froze in their tracks, but the children and dogs ran after it. The little wheel was way ahead of everyone and everything, going faster than the fire truck. Wheeler's teeth chattered, his hair stood on end, he squeaked and squealed in terror.

All the hamsters in the city who were neglected, not fed, or homeless heard Wheeler's desperate squeaks and squeals.

They crawled out from behind curtains, slipped out of mattresses, and jumped out from behind garbage cans to join him.

ALICE

SOME INCIDENTS IN THE LIFE OF A LITTLE GIRL OF
THE TWENTY-FIRST CENTURY, RECORDED BY HER
FATHER ON THE EVE OF HER FIRST DAY IN SCHOOL

By Kirill Bulychev
Translated and adapted by Mirra Ginsburg

Illustrated by Igor Galanin

MACMILLAN PUBLISHING CO., INC.
New York
COLLIER MACMILLAN PUBLISHERS
London

LIBRARY OF CONGRESS CATALOGING IN PUBLICATION DATA

Ginsburg, Mirra.
  Alice.

  Translated and adapted from K. Bulychev's Devochka s
kotoroĭ nichego ne sluchitsa, originally published in
Antologiīa sovetskoĭ fantastiki, Moscow, 1968.
  SUMMARY: Six stories about Alice, a five-year-old
living in the twenty-first century, and her adventures
with interplanetary visitors and strange animals.
  [1. Science fiction] I. Bulychev, Kirill Vsevolodovich.
Devochka s kotoroĭ nichego ne sluchitsa.
II. Galanin, I. III. Title.
PZ7.G43896Al   [Fic]   76–47539
ISBN 0–02–736520–4

EG

CONTENTS

Before long there were nearly a hundred of them, not counting guinea pigs. When they got to the main square they turned into a broad avenue and then, racing down a highway, they left the city behind them. Westward, toward the setting sun.

At the place where all the over- and underpasses
come together, all the busses, trucks, vans, and cars
had to stop because the hamster traffic was so heavy.

Not until the city lights had entirely disappeared from view did the hamsters stop in a corn field. Most of them were so tired out that they slept right in their little wheels, which had the advantage of being owl-proof.

Next morning they feasted on wheat. After laying in a supply of wheat in their cheek pouches, they set out once again.

They were last seen behind the big turnip field.
No one knows exactly where they all ran off to.
Probably some of them went back to their owners
because they were not used to finding their own food.

But most of them spread out over the countryside and are now living in wonderfully snug little holes that connect to secret winter storerooms.

One day a farmer found the discarded little wheels. He didn't want them in his field, so he drove his truck out to pick them up. As he was picking them up, an awful lot of hamsters were watching him.

And Wheeler, who still smelled faintly of cough
medicine and milk of magnesia, was one of them.